★ CAREERS IN THE US MILITARY

COMBAT EXPERTS

J. P. Miller

Rourke Educational Media

ROURKE'S SCHOOL to HOME CONNECTIONS
BEFORE AND DURING READING ACTIVITIES

Before Reading: *Building Background Knowledge and Vocabulary*

Building background knowledge can help children process new information and build upon what they already know. Before reading a book, it is important to tap into what children already know about the topic. This will help them develop their vocabulary and increase their reading comprehension.

Questions and Activities to Build Background Knowledge:

1. Look at the front cover of the book and read the title. What do you think this book will be about?
2. What do you already know about this topic?
3. Take a book walk and skim the pages. Look at the table of contents, photographs, captions, and bold words. Did these text features give you any information or predictions about what you will read in this book?

Vocabulary: *Vocabulary Is Key to Reading Comprehension*

Use the following directions to prompt a conversation about each word.

- Read the vocabulary words.
- What comes to mind when you see each word?
- What do you think each word means?

Vocabulary Words:
- ammunition
- combat
- first responders
- ordnance
- terrorist
- triage

During Reading: *Reading for Meaning and Understanding*

To achieve deep comprehension of a book, children are encouraged to use close reading strategies. During reading, it is important to have children stop and make connections. These connections result in deeper analysis and understanding of a book.

 ### Close Reading a Text

During reading, have children stop and talk about the following:

- Any confusing parts
- Any unknown words
- Text to text, text to self, text to world connections
- The main idea in each chapter or heading

Encourage children to use context clues to determine the meaning of any unknown words. These strategies will help children learn to analyze the text more thoroughly as they read.

When you are finished reading this book, turn to the next-to-last page for **After-Reading Questions** and an **Activity**.

TABLE OF CONTENTS

The Importance of Combat...................4
Combat as Work..................................8
Nerves of Steel.................................28
Memory Game....................................30
Index..31
After-Reading Questions....................31
Activity..31
About the Author...............................32

THE IMPORTANCE OF COMBAT

Combat Experts are the most-skilled members of the United States military that go to war. Most are carefully chosen for their job. Combat Experts are leaders in protecting the United States against its enemies. Most of the time, their work is top-secret.

NINUS MILLER
Infantry soldiers such as Ninus Miller, shown here, have been part of the United States Army since 1775.

combat (KAHM-bat):
fighting between people or armies

The US military is one of the best in the world. Its different branches are the Army, Air Force, Navy, Marines, and Coast Guard. Combat Experts in each branch are trained and prepared to fight to protect the United States. They are the first to go fight in wars.

COMBAT AS WORK

A group of Combat Experts will often possess many different jobs. They all work together. One kind of Combat Expert is combat photographers. They use video, photo cameras, and audio equipment to document war images.

Combat photographers help keep the public informed in times of war and peace. They can give people important information during natural disasters. A combat photographer tells the story of what happened through pictures. They go anywhere and everywhere that military units go.

To do well as a combat photographer, it is important to have an interest in art. You must like telling stories through pictures. Combat photographers must also be in good physical shape. They must stay strong for battle and be quick to catch the action with their equipment.

READY AT ALL TIMES

A Combat Photographer doesn't stay behind a camera. They must be ready to fight in combat at all times. That sometimes means using weapons.

Things can be scary when a military unit is under attack. Smoke fills the air, and it can be hard to breathe and see. That's when Combat Medics make it to the scene. Their hearts race as fast as their feet. They must search the area for dangers such as explosives before they can help anyone. Combat Medics are the military's emergency **first responders**. They save US military members injured in war.

GREAT STRENGTH

A Combat Medic must be very strong. They carry over 30 pounds (13.6 kilograms) of military gear plus a weapon. They also must be strong enough to carry an injured person to safety.

first responders (furst ri-SPAHN-durz): people whose job is to respond first in an emergency, such as police officers, firefighters, or paramedics

Just like Emergency Medical Technicians (EMTs) in your local community, Combat Medics save lives. They set up a **triage** to treat injured people. Next, Combat Medics turn the most seriously wounded over to the Aeromedical Evacuation Team to be flown to the nearest military hospital.

To do well as a Combat Medic, it is important to be able to think fast in stressful situations. Combat Medics first attend basic military training. After that, they attend special medical and survival training.

LIFELIKE TRAINING

Combat Medics must have regular specialized training. Sometimes they use lifelike models. The models are programmed to bleed from fake gunshot wounds and other combat injuries.

triage (TREE-ahj): an area that gives medical treatments to patients depending on how badly they are injured

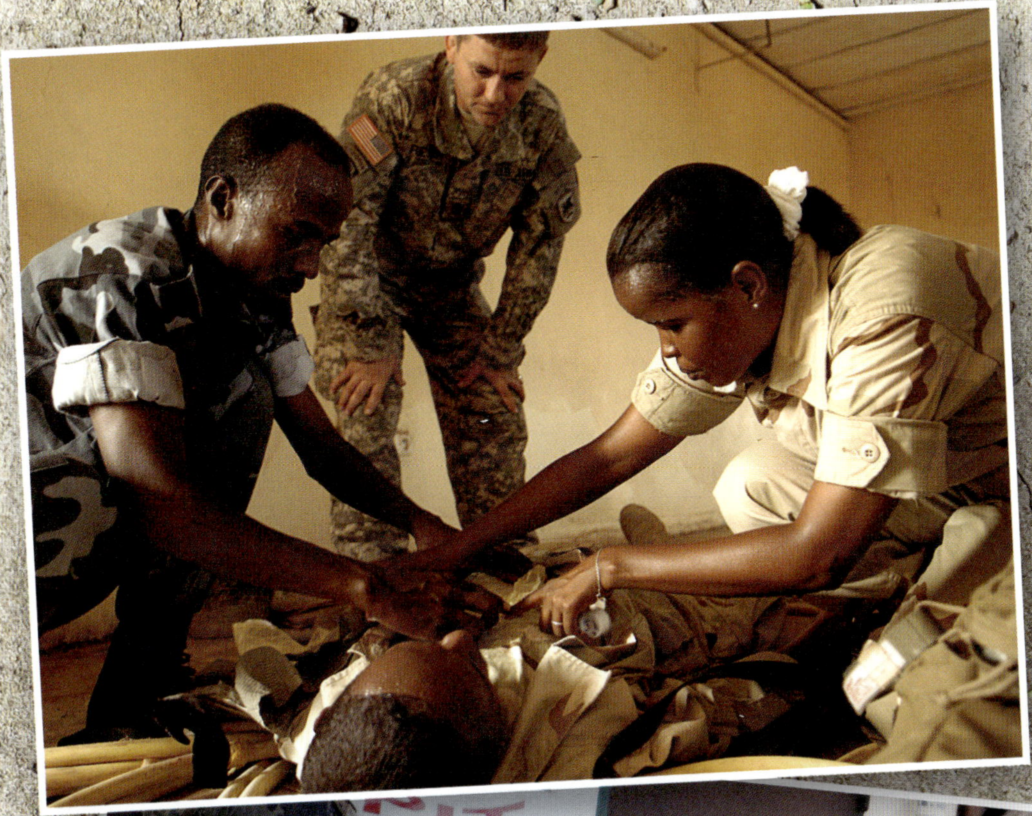

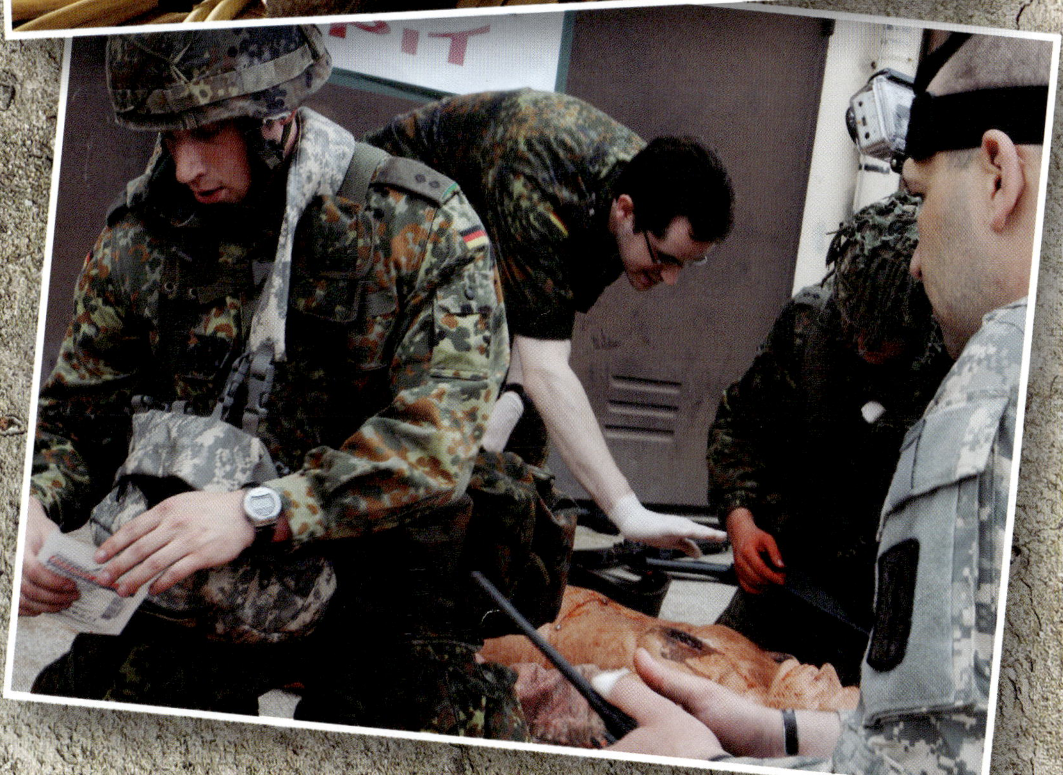

15

Some Combat Experts have very specific jobs. One such job is as an Osprey helicopter pilot. They fly other Combat Experts, equipment, and supplies all around the world. These pilots also fly White House staff around Washington, DC, and make other important flights. Osprey flights can take hours.

FUEL IN THE SKY

How does a helicopter refuel if it is too dangerous to land? It happens while the helicopter is flying! Osprey pilots are trained to carefully connect their helicopter to another aircraft to refuel on long trips. This process is very dangerous to both pilots if not done correctly.

To do well as an Osprey pilot, it is important to stay calm at all times. A pilot must be alert when flying, especially when they are in war zones. Being a pilot also requires a lot of training. Pilots first attend officer's military training and then go to flight school.

> "Sometimes, there's a job that simply must be done. It will be extremely challenging but must be done regardless."
> — Edmond L. Hooks Jr., Captain, Marines, MV-22 Osprey Pilot

Below the water line of some Navy ships are **Ordnance** Specialists hard at work. Here, they build bombs, rockets, and missiles. This is the **ammunition** used in war. A different crew loads the ammunition onto fighter jets.

If a weapon or ammunition is not used by a certain time after it is made, it is dangerous. It can fail to work or even blow up. It must be destroyed so no one gets hurt. An Ordnance Specialist uses special equipment to blow up old and unwanted weapons and ammunition.

LIKE GIANT BULLETS

Many missiles are shaped like bullets, only much larger. They are 10 to 12 inches (25 to 30 centimeters) thick and up 20 feet (six meters) long.

ammunition (am-yuh-NISH-uhn): things such as bullets or shells that can be fired from weapons

ordnance (ORD-nans): the part of the military that works with weapons and combat equipment

To be an Ordnance Specialist, you should be able to stay calm at all times at work. You must be comfortable working with dangerous things. You also must like to study! Ordnance Specialists have nearly ten months of training after they finish basic training.

> "To work in ordnance, your head always has to be on a swivel."
> — Joseph F. Whitmire, Gunnery Officer, Navy (Retired), Warrant Officer 4

Some of the most important jobs in the US military are top-secret. Military members of the Special Forces are important because they are hand-picked Combat Experts. They carry out very specific assignments. They cannot tell anyone about their plans or training. Their missions can be very dangerous. People could be injured or killed if others learned this secret information.

A Special Forces member can have many different responsibilities. They carried out many jobs when the Special Forces SEAL Team Six helped capture Osama bin Laden, the leader of a **terrorist** group. Special Forces members planned the top-secret attack on his hidden base for over a year. They built a model of the base. Sometimes they practiced going through it wearing blindfolds in case there would be no light inside. There was no room for mistakes.

terrorist (TER-ur-ist): someone who uses violence and threats in order to, for example, frighten people, obtain power, or force a government to do something

To succeed as a member of the Special Forces, you have to be able to handle stress. You must work very hard. Special Forces members can be experts in things such as long-distance shooting, and they are the best at what they do.

Being a Special Forces member requires a lot of training. Combat Experts first attend basic military training. After that, they have special training in swimming, parachuting, and survival.

A SELECT GROUP

Special Forces members have to be good at making decisions quickly. They have to be ready to leave for a mission on a moment's notice. Only a select group of people are able to fill these roles.

NERVES OF STEEL

Combat Experts perform many dangerous jobs. They have a lot of special training. They work with weapons, ammunition, and even cameras to do their jobs. Everything they do prepares them for the danger of the battlefield.

Are you brave? Can you make decisions quickly and stay calm around dangerous things? If so, you might be a good Combat Expert.

MEMORY GAME

Look at the pictures. What do you remember reading on the pages where each image appeared?

INDEX

medic(s) 12, 14
military branches 6
Osprey 16, 18
photographer(s) 8, 10
rockets 20
SEAL Team Six 24
Special Forces 24, 26
weapons 10, 12, 20, 28

AFTER-READING QUESTIONS

1. What are Combat Experts?
2. What are the branches of the military?
3. Why is it important for Special Forces to ensure their job duties remain top-secret?
4. What are two ways that Osprey helicopters are used?
5. Why are some bombs and rockets destroyed?

ACTIVITY

Can you find your way through your home in the dark? Using a piece of graph or notebook paper, draw the floor plan of your home. Label each room, door, and window. Practice going through your house from memory in the dark like the Special Forces Team does on their missions.

ABOUT THE AUTHOR

J. P. is a veteran of the United States Air Force living in Metro Atlanta, Georgia. She now writes children's books that augment a child's classroom experience. J. P. is very excited to combine her love for writing with her military experience to produce the *Careers in the US Military* series.

© 2021 Rourke Educational Media

All rights reserved. No part of this book may be reproduced or utilized in any form or by any means, electronic or mechanical including photocopying, recording, or by any information storage and retrieval system without permission in writing from the publisher.

www.rourkeeducationalmedia.com

Quote sources: Edmond L. Hooks Jr., interview by author. Joseph F. Whitmire, interview by author.

PHOTO CREDITS: page 4: ©Paul W. Miller; page 5: ©VP_90 / Shutterstock(background); page 5: ©Danita Delimont Photography / Newscom(top); page 5: ©Rena Schild / Shutterstock(bottom); page 7: ©StockPhotosLV / Shutterstock; page 9: ©Pfc. Rashene Mincy / defense.gov; page 11: ©Lance Cpl. Juanenrique Owings / U.S. Marine Corp; page 13: ©ANURAKE SINGTO-ON / Shutterstock; page 15: ©Kurt Kaiser / Wikimedia(background); page 15: ©U.S. Army / Wikimedia(top); page 15: ©U.S. Army / Wikimedia(bottom); page 17: ©Stefan Bocchino / U.S. Air Force; page 19: ©Paul Vinten / Shutterstock(background); page 19: ©VanderWolf-Images / Getty Images(top); page 19: ©Kyodo / Newscom(bottom); page 21: ©U.S. Navy/Sipa USA / Newscom; page 23: ©Sgt. Michael T. Crawford / U.S. Army; page 25: ©Chris Desmond/ZUMA Press / Newscom; page 27: ©Olmez / Shutterstock(background); page 27: ©Getmilitaryphotos / Shutterstock(top); page 27: ©Msgt. Jeffrey Allen/ZUMA Press / Newscom(bottom); page 29: ©Jayme Pastoric/ZUMA Press / Newscom

Edited by: Tracie Santos
Cover and interior design by: Alison Tracey

Library of Congress PCN Data

Combat Experts / J. P. Miller
(Careers in the US Military)
ISBN 978-1-73164-355-1 (hard cover)(alk. paper)
ISBN 978-1-73164-319-3 (soft cover)
ISBN 978-1-73164-387-2 (e-Book)
ISBN 978-1-73164-419-0 (ePub)
Library of Congress Control Number: 2020945265

Rourke Educational Media
Printed in the United States of America
01-3502011937